The Montessori White Papers

Volume 2

Laura Flores Shaw, Editor

DEDICATION

This volume is dedicated to all Montessori practitioners.

CONTENTS

CONTRIBUTORS

AUTHORS

Dr. Deborah Ely Budding is a board certified neuropsychologist who works with children, adolescents, and adults in the Los Angeles area. She is co-author of *Subcortical Structures and Cognition: Implications for Neuropsychological Assessment*, which was published in 2008, as well as peer-reviewed articles related to subcortical contributions to cognitive and emotional function. Dr. Budding is a supervising faculty member at Harbor-UCLA's neuropsychology training program and is increasingly involved in research involving transcranial direct current stimulation (tDCS). She has a particular interest in the cerebellum's contributions to non-motor function, in brain-behavior relationships in neurodevelopmental disorders, and in finding ways to amplify the voices of women and people of color in science education.

Dr. Jacqueline Cossentino is the Senior Associate and Director of Research for the National Center for Montessori in the Public Sector. Jackie's Montessori career began as a parent, and quickly evolved into researcher and administrator, as well as university professor. An ethnographer by training, since 2001 she has drawn from her direct experience as head of an independent Montessori school and principal of a large, urban public Montessori school to produce an internationally recognized body of scholarship on Montessori education. Jackie's 26 years in education have included roles as a middle and high school English teacher, an elementary school principal, a professional developer for schools, districts, and museums, and a professor of educational leadership at the University of Maryland. Currently Jackie is a Lecturer in Loyola Maryland's Montessori Studies program. She serves on the boards of Montessori Northwest and the Montessori Charter Management Organization. She received a B.A. in History from Smith College and an M.Ed. and Ed.D. from the Harvard Graduate School of Education.

Laura Flores Shaw is the lead editor, writer, and founder of White Paper Press, a think tank specializing in translating scientific research into terms that allows people to make informed decisions about their lives. She holds bachelors and master degrees in psychology and is currently a doctoral candidate in education with a specialization in mind, brain, and teaching at

Johns Hopkins University School of Education. Laura previously worked as a family therapist in the public school system where she realized her desire to work on the prevention rather than intervention side of mental health. That led her to reviving a failing Montessori school where she became passionate about creating environments that allow children to thrive in every way. In 2014, she retired from school administration to focus on advocating at a broader level for frameworks that can improve the lives of children and their families. She currently writes, speaks, and consults internationally on education, brain development, and parenting.

ADVISORY EDITORS

Dr. Kay M. Baker is currently the Director of Training for the AMI Elementary Course for children ages 6-12 at the Montessori Institute of San Diego. Her academic qualifications include a bachelor's degree in mathematics, a master's and Ph.D. in mathematics education and AMI diplomas for children ages 3-6 and 6-12. Dr. Baker is also an AMI consultant for primary and elementary classes. She has given many talks and workshops nationally and internationally on topics ranging from the four planes of development to suitable classroom practices. Dr. Baker is particularly interested in children's thinking, having investigated children's solution strategies for multiplication word problems for her doctoral dissertation. She has spent her career considering the necessity for adults to continue to learn in order to aid the life of the child throughout development.

Dr. Annette Haines is an internationally recognized lecturer, examiner, consultant and trainer of the Association Montessori Internationale (AMI). She has been involved in the field of Montessori education since 1972 and has extensive background in the Children's House classroom. Dr. Haines holds both AMI Primary and Elementary Diplomas. Additionally, she has a Bachelor of Arts degree in English literature from Washington University, a Masters Degree in Education from Cleveland State University, and a Doctorate in Education from Southern Illinois University-Edwardsville with research focused on concentration and normalization within the Montessori Prepared Environment. Annette is the chair of the Scientific Pedagogy Group and the Material Committee of the AMI. She is also a member of the AMI Global Research Committee and currently chairs the recently formed Stewarding Council for AMI in the United States. Her articles have been published in the AMI Communications, the NAMTA Journal, Montessori Talks to Parents, and elsewhere around the globe.

Dr. Jayme Jones is a pediatric neuropsychologist. She received her BA in psychology from UCI and her PhD in clinical psychology from the University of Kansas. She then completed additional training at both LAC-USC and Harbor-UCLA Medical Centers. Currently, Dr. Jones provides neuropsychological evaluation, individual and family consultation and psychodynamically oriented psychotherapy to children, adolescents, and adults. She has an extensive background in the assessment and treatment of pre-school and early school-aged children who have a variety of neurodevelopmental and psychiatric disorders such as Autism, Asperger's, ADHD, learning disorders, mood disorders, and anxiety disorders. Dr. Jones has a particular interest in the impact of trauma on development and is also an expert in the treatment of traumatic crises and loss in both adults and children. Dr. Jones also assesses children with regard to the effects of mild to moderate traumatic brain injuries, seizures, and endocrine and metabolic disorders.

INTRODUCTION

In this second volume of *The Montessori White Papers*, a variety of themes are discussed to further broaden the public's understanding of Montessori and to articulate the scientific research that supports the work of Montessori educators around the world. As always, these papers present science and Montessori in plain language.

Reading and the Brain, Part 1: Developing the Reading Circuit outlines how reading is taught in Montessori, how those strategies correlate with recent reading research, and how the brain is changed through development and connections of disparate brain areas. This paper begins the discussion around the need to develop automatic behaviors necessary for later learning. *Born to Move, Part 1: Movement and Cognition*, the third paper in this volume, continues that discussion by explaining the link between movement and cognition and explaining why an educational environment rich in sensorimotor materials is necessary to train automatic movements required for executive functions development.

Montessori Schools Help Children Exposed to Trauma articulates the various stress levels that children are often exposed to and explains how the Montessori environment, with its concern for the whole child, helps children exposed to toxic stress develop capacities for resilience and self-reliance.

Play is a constant theme in mainstream media with respect to early childhood education; however, the construct of play is rarely defined or examined. *Montessori and Play* uses the scholarly literature to break down this construct and compares it with the children's work in their Montessori classrooms, dispelling the false dichotomy of work and play.

Finally, a white paper (*Education for the 21st Century Economy*) published in Volume 1 of this series proposed that Montessori is *the* educational method for developing the skills necessary to be successful in the 21st century knowledge economy. *Montessori and the Systems Worldview*, however, argues that there is an even more important reason why Montessori is *the* educational method for the 21st century: Montessori education fosters a systems view of the world, which is necessary for the sustainability of our planet and, hence, our species.

Throughout these and our previously published white papers, a common theme emerges: Dr. Maria Montessori was clearly ahead of her time in her thinking about education, human development, and global society. As both an educator and a parent, I am most grateful for her brilliance and foresight.

Laura Flores Shaw
Founder, Editor, Writer
White Paper Press

READING AND THE BRAIN, PART 1: DEVLOPING THE READING CIRCUIT

Laura Flores Shaw, MS

KEY POINTS

- Unlike language, there is no innate "reading circuit" in the brain. Reading requires specific training to connect two different brain regions: the object recognition system, which allows us to identify objects and faces, and the language circuit, which enables us to learn any language.[1,6]

- Montessori provides auditory training through spoken language, reading aloud, language games, and sensorial materials to help develop what researchers call phonemic awareness – awareness of sounds in spoken language without any visual cue of letters.[5,12] Phonemic awareness is necessary for later reading skills.[14]

- Research shows that mapping sounds to individual letters leads to better reading.[1,9,17] Research also shows that learning letter sounds through touch rather than just seeing how a letter is written leads to better decoding and later reading skills.[7]

- The visual system of beginning readers sees words as if they are whole objects;[19] thus it is necessary to train the object recognition system for visual acuity. Montessori does this.

- Through interaction with all of the primary classrooms materials, the child's brain is literally changed, and a new reading circuit is developed.

READING AND THE BRAIN, PART 1: DEVLOPING THE READING CIRCUIT

Laura Flores Shaw, MS

It was very hard for me to learn how to read. It did not seem logical for the letter m to be called em, and yet with some vowel following it you did not say ema but ma. It was impossible for me to read that way. At last, when I went to the Montessori school, the teacher did not teach me the names of the consonants but the sounds. In this way I could read the first book I found in a dirty chest in the storeroom of the house.

Gabriel García Márquez
Living to Tell the Tale

During my tenure as head of a Montessori school, parents often asked questions related to reading. A common concern was, "My child doesn't know her abc's! Why doesn't she know her abc's?"

Because we all grew up learning to sing our abc's and few of us remember how we actually learned to read, we assume that naming the letters of the alphabet is evidence that a child "knows her letters." In actuality, it is only evidence that she knows the *names* of the letters, which actually doesn't help her learn to read. In fact, knowing the names of letters without knowing their corresponding *sounds* may actually delay reading.[1]

The "reading wars" have also contributed to our confusion about how best to teach reading. These wars began in the mid-nineteenth century when education reformer Horace Mann argued that forcing children to learn the sounds of the letters was ridiculous as letters are "bloodless, ghostly apparitions" (p. 89).[2] Sounds like someone didn't enjoy learning his phonics! Instead, he proposed that children should learn to read whole words. Since then, education has been debating the best way to teach reading to children, and the debate has essentially been polarized between phonics and whole language learning (where children memorize how a word looks on paper).[3,4]

The real issue at the heart of this war is whether or not reading is a natural, "hard-wired" process similar to learning to speak.[1] Whole language proponents claim that it is, while phonics proponents claim that it's not. Research shows that phonics proponents are right – at least with respect to decoding letters (phonics proponents have views about comprehension that aren't so right, but we'll discuss that in another paper in our next volume).[1,4,5]

According to neuroscientist Stanislas Dehaene, while we have evolved to be born to speak, we haven't evolved to the point of being born to read. There simply is no innate "reading circuit" in the brain in the same way that there is a language circuit. Ultimately, reading requires specific training to connect two different brain regions: the object recognition system, which allows us to identify objects and faces, and the language circuit, which enables us to learn any language.[1,6]

So while conventional educators engaged, and in some respects continue to engage, in the reading wars, Montessorians have spent the last hundred-plus years quietly preparing and guiding students toward reading using methods necessary to connect the object recognition system and the language circuit.[1,7,8,9]

HOW MONTESSORI TEACHES READING
Awareness of Sounds

According to Montessori, to prepare a child to read, you must first

> ...train the child's attention to follow sounds and noises which are produced in the environment, to recognize them and to discriminate between them, [this] is to prepare his attention to follow more accurately the sounds of articulate language (p. 123).[10]

Training a child to differentiate sounds begins at birth and naturally occurs through exposure to language in conversation, being read to, singing songs, and word games such as The Sound Game where a teacher holds an object in her hand (e.g., a glass) and says, "I'm thinking of something that starts with /g/, what is it?"[11] Dr. Montessori also specifically instructed teachers to "pronounce clearly and completely the sounds" of words when speaking or singing songs to the children (p. 123).[10]

The Sensorial materials in the primary classroom are also designed to train the children's awareness of sounds. The Bells, for instance, are used to help the children distinguish the different notes through matching and other activities long before the children begin to learn the names of those musical notes. The Sound Cylinders, which are filled with different materials to create various types of sounds when the children shake them, also train auditory discrimination as the children try to match those different sounds.[11]

All this auditory training helps develop what researchers call phonemic awareness – awareness of sounds in spoken language without any visual cue of letters.[5,12] There is evidence that poor phonemic awareness predicts later poor reading ability.[13] And meta-analyses examining the body of research specific to phonemic awareness have shown a causal link between it and reading skills.[14] Thus, researchers suggest that learning phonics – the process of matching sounds to letter symbols – alone is not enough. Activities that develop the awareness of sounds in language without any letter representation of those sounds should also be provided.[5] Montessori provides a rich variety of such activities.

Learning Letters Through Touch

Conventional education generally begins teaching the children to map the sounds to individual letters (phonics) around age five. Montessori, however, begins phonics learning around age three.[11] The method also uses a multisensory approach, which is not used in conventional classrooms.

As a child traces a cursive Sandpaper Letter with his fingers in the same way he would write it, he says its sound aloud.[11] Researchers refer to this approach as "multisensory trace," and it was successfully used by educational psychologist Grace Fernald, who was inspired by the work of physician Édouard Séguin and Maria Montessori,[15] in the early twentieth century to help struggling readers.[16] In fact, the method is still used today for students with learning disabilities.

Interestingly, Fernald's multi-sensory method is a whole language approach where children trace whole words rather than individual phonemes. But the research shows that it's ultimately the decoding of words through individual letters that leads to better reading, as this skill allows children to decode never before seen words.[1,9,17]

Additionally, research examining the effects of multisensory trace shows that it's more effective than merely showing a child a letter and saying its sound.[18] In fact, researchers confirmed that it's the *act of touching* and not just seeing how the letter is written that leads to better decoding and later reading skills.[7] Ultimately, it's the combined visual, auditory, and tactile experience that allows a child to learn her phonics so she can decode words. And, of course, Montessori knew this:

> There develop, contemporaneously, three sensations when the directress *shows the letter* to the child and has him trace it; the visual sensation, the tactile sensation, and the muscular sensation. In this way the *image of the graphic sign* is fixed in a much shorter space of time than when it was, according to ordinary methods, acquired only through the visual image (pp. 276-277; emphasis in original).[11]

Visual Acuity Training

But Montessori does more than help children become aware of the sounds of language and then map those sounds to letters. The method also deliberately trains the brain's object recognition system to discriminate the subtle differences of shapes. The Geometry Cabinet, which is comprised of various wooden two-dimensional geometric shapes fitted within frames like puzzle pieces, are used to develop visual acuity (in addition to learning the shapes' names).[11] As the child traces the contours of each shape while saying its name, she learns to discern the subtle differences between, say, an obtuse and an equilateral triangle.

As it turns out, training for visual acuity makes complete sense. The visual system of beginning readers sees words as if they are whole objects.[19] Thus, the system needs to be trained to see the individual parts that comprise the whole picture. Interestingly, studies show that readers who have spent many hours learning to discern individual letters can better perceive geometric shapes than people who cannot read.[20,21] This suggests that visual acuity is a general skill; thus, training to perceive subtle differences in geometric shapes helps to train the visual system to see the subtle differences of letters like d/b/p. And we know from studies of illiterate adults that such perceptional training needs to be explicit, as it doesn't occur simply through maturation.[20]

Writing Before Reading

Once a child has learned most of her letters, she can begin to write with the help of the Moveable Alphabet. Using these large, beautiful cursive letters, children can spell out words that interest them. Of course, they spell them phonetically, but proper spelling is not a concern at this early stage of language exploration. However, because they are phonetically spelling out their words, their phonics knowledge is reinforced, helping them to eventually become expert decoders. As Dr. Montessori stated:

> When a child in our school knows how to write, *he knows how to read the sounds of which the word is composed* (p. 297; emphasis in original).[11]

Meanwhile, the child has also been preparing her hand to write with an actual pencil since toddlerhood, manipulating puzzles with knobs to develop her pincer grasp. The Geometry Cabinet and Metal Insets are also used to refine the ability to effectively handle a writing instrument before actually writing letters by hand. All of the Practical Life exercises have also been training the children to do things in sequence from left to right, just as we do in writing and reading. Later on, the child will begin to write sentences with the Moveable Alphabet and copy those sentences onto lined paper – again, knowing to do so from left to right. The act of writing out words also reinforces the child's mastery of letter sounds.[22]

Reading!

Finally, the teacher will offer the Phonetic Object Game. The teacher will take a basket of objects and spread them out on the table. She will then write down the name of the object she is thinking of on a small slip of paper. As she hands that slip to the child, the teacher asks, "What do you see?" The child will begin to sound out the word, and the teacher will encourage him to say it faster until the word "bursts upon his consciousness" (p. 298).[11]

And, thus, the child begins to perceive himself as a reader.

THE BRAIN IS CHANGED

Learning to read is an unnatural process requiring explicit training, which the Montessori method provides. However, the training described herein is only a general outline of a very complex process that is supported both indirectly and directly by all of the materials in the primary (3-6 year-old) classroom. And it is through interaction with all of these materials that the child's brain is literally changed. A new reading circuit is developed through a massive number of connections between the objection recognition and language systems, and the child gains, as neuroscientist Dehaene states, "the ability to access the spoken language system through vision (p. 7).[6] And this, according to Montessori, gives the child the keys to world.[23]

References

1. Dehaene, S. (2009). *Reading in the brain: The new science of how we read*. New York, NY: Viking.

2. Kim, J. S. (2008). Research and reading wars. In F. M. Hess (Ed.), *When research matters: How scholarship influences education policy* (pp. 89-111). Cambrdige, MA: Harvard Education Press.

3. Pearson, P. D. (2004). The reading wars. *Educational Policy, 18*(1), 216-252.

4. Moats, L. (2007). Whole language hijinks: Thomas B. Fordham Institute.

5. Lonigan, C., Schatschneider, C., Westberg, L., & The National Early Literacy Panel. (2008). Identification of children's skills and abilities linked to later outcomes in reading, writing, and spelling. In N. E. L. Panel (Ed.), *Developing early literacy: A scientific synthesis of early literacy*

development and implications for intervention (pp. 55-105). Jessups, ML: National Institute for Literacy & The Partnership for Reading.

6. Dehaene, S. (2013). Inside the letterbox: How literacy transforms the human brain. *Cerebrum: the Dana Forum on Brain Science, 2013*, 7.

7. Bara, F., Gentaz, E., Colé, P., & Sprenger-Charolles, L. (2004). The visuo-haptic and haptic exploration of letters increases the kindergarten-children's understanding of the alphabetic principle. *Cognitive Development, 19*(3), 433-449. doi: http://dx.doi.org/10.1016/j.cogdev.2004.05.003

8. Gentaz, E., Sprenger-Charolles, L., & Theurel, A. (2015). Differences in the predictors of reading comprehension in first graders from low socio-economic status families with either good or poor decoding skills. *PLoS ONE, 10*(3), 1-16. doi: 10.1371/journal.pone.0119581

9. Yoncheva, Y. N., Wise, J., & McCandliss, B. (2015). Hemispheric specialization for visual words is shaped by attention to sublexical units during initial learning. *Brain and Language, 145–146*(0), 23-33. doi: http://dx.doi.org/10.1016/j.bandl.2015.04.001

10. Montessori, M. (1965). *Dr. Montessori's own handbook*. New York, NY: Schocken Books.

11. Montessori, M. (2013). *The Montessori method*. New Brunswick, NJ: Transaction Publishers.

12. Ehri, L. C. (1987). Learning to read and spell words. *Journal of Literacy Research, 19*(1), 5-31.

13. Ziegler, J. C., & Goswami, U. (2005). Reading acquisition, developmental dyslexia, and skilled reading across languages: a psycholinguistic grain size theory. *Psychological Bulletin, 131*(1), 3. ; White-Schwoch, T., Woodruff Carr, K., Thompson, E. C., Anderson, S., Nicol, T., Bradlow, A. R., . . . Kraus, N. (2015). Auditory processing in noise: A preschool biomarker for literacy. *PLOS Biology, 13*(7), e1002196. doi: 10.1371/journal.pbio.1002196

14. Bus, A. G., & van Ijzendoorn, M. H. (1999). Phonological awareness and early reading: A meta-analysis of experimental training studies. *Journal of Educational Psychology, 91*(3), 403-414. doi: 10.1037/0022-0663.91.3.403; Melby-Lervåg, M., Lyster, S.-A. H., & Hulme, C. (2012). Phonological skills and their role in learning to read: A meta-analytic review. *Psychological Bulletin, 138*(2), 322-352. doi: 10.1037/a002674410.1037/a0026744.supp (Supplemental)

15. Loudon, B., & Arthur, G. (1940). An application of the Fernald method to an extreme case of reading disability. *The Elementary School Journal, 40*(8), 599-606. doi: 10.2307/997845

16. Fernald, G. M., & Keller, H. (1921). The effect of kinaesthetic factors in the development of word recognition in the case of non-readers. *The Journal of Educational Research, 4*(5), 355-377. doi: 10.2307/27524563

17. Ehri, L. C. (1998). Grapheme—Phoneme knowledge is essential for learning to read words in English. In J. L. Metsala & L. C. Ehri (Eds.), *Word recognition in beginning literacy* (pp. 3-40). New York, NY: Routledge; Ehri, L. C., Nunes, S. R., Stahl, S. A., & Willows, D. M. (2001). Systematic phonics instruction helps students learn to read: Evidence from the National Reading Panel's meta-analysis. *Review of Educational Research, 71*(3), 393-447.

18. Gentaz, E., Colé, P., & Bara, F. (2003). Évaluation d'entraînements multi-sensoriels de préparation à la lecture pour les enfants en grande section de maternelle: Une étude sur la contribution du système haptique manuel. *L'année Psychologique, 103*(4), 561-584. As cited in Bara, et al (2004).

19. Frith, U. (1985). Beneath the surface of developmental dyslexia. In K. Patterson, J. Marshall & M. Coltheart (Eds.), *Surface dyslexia: Neuropyschological and cognitive studies of phonological reading* (pp. 301-330). London: Eribaum; Navon, D. (1977). Forest before trees: The precedence of global features in visual perception. *Cognitive psychology, 9*(3), 353-383.

20. Kolinsky, R., Morais, J., & Verhaeghe, A. (1994). Visual separability: A study on unschooled adults. *Perception, 23*, 471-471.

21. Kolinsky, R., Morais, J., Content, A., & Cary, L. (1987). Finding parts within figures: A developmental study. *Perception, 16*(3), 399-407.

22. Bara, F., & Gentaz, E. (2011). Haptics in teaching handwriting: The role of perceptual and visuo-motor skills. *Human Movement Science, 30*(4), 745-759. doi: http://dx.doi.org/10.1016/j.humov.2010.05.015

23. Montessori, M. (1967). *The absorbent mind* (1st ed.). New York: Holt, Rinehart and Winston.

MONTESSORI SCHOOLS HELP CHILDREN EXPOSED TO TRAUMA

Jacqueline Cossentino, EdD

KEY POINTS

- Most of us think of trauma as singular, horrifying events like natural disasters, school shootings, or catastrophic accidents. But chronic traumatic situations are much more common: domestic violence, mental illness, substance abuse, or imprisonment of adult household members.

- Ongoing, unaddressed trauma triggers multiple stress-related networks, which activates the flight/fight/freeze safety response. When these stress-related networks become hypersensitive, the child enters a state of arousal even when no threat is present.[5,6]

- In these moments, it is important to remember that the child is not "thinking." Rather, she is reacting automatically, so more important than talking is a physical means of calming down.

- With their emphasis on movement, purposeful exploration, self-correction, and mindfulness, Montessori environments turn out to be ideal settings for developing long-term capacities for resilience and self-reliance.[3,8]

MONTESSORI SCHOOLS HELP CHILDREN EXPOSED TO TRAUMA

Jacqueline Cossentino, EdD

The implementation of any educational system ought to begin with the creation of an environment that protects the child from the difficult and dangerous obstacles that threaten him in the adult world.

Maria Montessori
The Child in the Family

When most of us think of trauma in schools, we think of singular, horrifying events like natural disasters, school shootings, or catastrophic accidents. In these cases, schools spring into action: time is set aside to process the impact of the event, counselors are deployed to speak with children, families are directed to local resources for addressing anxiety and grief, and both teachers and families are informed of how to respond to signs of post traumatic stress disorder (PTSD). The entire organism shifts its focus to attentive care, healing, and love.

That's because educators understand that traumatic events have profound impact on everyone associated with them. Feelings of terror and helplessness linger long after the event, disrupting learning, social life and, most significantly, development. But chronic traumatic situations are much more common. And, though lacking the drama of acute events, because they are ongoing, they have even greater impact, especially on the developing brain.

Often referred to as Adverse Childhood Experiences (ACE), a range of circumstances – from household dysfunction (which includes experiences such as domestic violence, mental illness, substance abuse, or imprisonment of adult household members) to extreme neglect and physical, emotional or sexual abuse – produce intense feelings of fear, guilt, shame, and loss of trust in others. Children who experience these types of trauma are much more likely to suffer long-term difficulties such as depression, substance abuse, even suicide.[1]

And chances are excellent that any classroom in the US includes children who have experienced these kinds of trauma. That's because adverse experiences like exposure to substance abuse, household violence, and neglect don't discriminate according to income, level of education, or ethnicity. Schools, in general, aren't as effective at responding to chronic stress as they are to acute events. Montessori schools, however, are, by design, more likely to meet the needs of families who have experienced trauma because they view children holistically and because Montessori naturally incorporates activities that are similar to the practice of mindfulness,[2] which research has shown increases wellbeing.[3]

STRESS AND HUMAN DEVELOPMENT

Early childhood trauma, it turns out, can do damage not just to feelings, but to the very structure of the developing brain.[4] Ongoing, unaddressed trauma triggers multiple stress-related networks, which activates the flight/fight/freeze safety response. When these stress-related networks become hypersensitive, the child enters a state of arousal even when no threat is present.[5,6]

Studies have shown that some children who have been exposed to severe, prolonged trauma have changes in their brains, including a smaller amygdala and hippocampus; both structures play a role in emotion and memory. Children with hypersensitive flight/fight/freeze responses can have difficulty with self-regulation and concentration, which can result in learning and behavioral challenges.

We see a mild version of this stress response whenever a child trantrums. Often triggered by an unfulfilled desire – the doll her friend is currently playing with, the ice cream cone just before dinner, the bath she cannot avoid – trantrums can appear to be the work of a willful, undisciplined child (and, to be fair, sometimes they are). But sometimes, they are the result of a mind that cannot distinguish between wants and needs and whose body, therefore, perceives the unmet want/need as danger. The result is behavior that is driven by the brain's most primitive instinct to survive: the stress hormone cortisol is released, the heart races, pupils dilate, muscles tense, breathing shortens. It's scary for the child and, often, just as scary for the parent or caregiver, as it can trigger our own stress response, which makes the situation escalate.

As young children learn to discern needs from wants, tantrums usually give way to more regulated ways of communicating. As adults, we can support the growth of effective self-regulation in two key ways. First is by helping them, in the short term, cope when they are confronted with severe stress. Second is by allowing them to develop self-regulation skills necessary for long-term resilience.

FROM SURVIVAL TO THINKING

When people are in the midst of a full-blown stress response, their ability to do anything other than survive is greatly diminished. That's one reason why reasoning with a tantruming toddler doesn't work. At that moment, rather, what the child needs is to calm down and re-regulate. When a child is in fight or flight mode, step one is to assure safety. We do that by using a soft voice to (a) validate the child's feelings ("I can see you are frustrated") and (b) letting the child know that we will not abandon him or her ("I'm going to stay close by") while also acknowledging that the child needs space ("is it OK if I come closer?"). Sometimes the need for space may be fulfilled by providing a "break" in a quiet part of the room.

It is important to remember that in these moments, the child is not "thinking." Rather, she is reacting automatically, so more important than talking is a physical means of calming down. Activities such as bouncing on a yoga ball, squeezing a stress ball, walking on the line, taking a run outside, jumping rope, or playing with a Hula Hoop can help restore equilibrium. When a child is no longer in fight/flight/freeze she can better access thoughtful, intentional behavior. The figure below depicts the process from survival to thinking.

HEALTHY STRESS, MINDFULNESS, AND MONTESSORI

Everyone experiences stress, and when those experiences are ongoing and unaddressed, they become toxic. And while the results of toxic stress are severe and lasting, when trauma and its attending stress are addressed sensitively, people, especially children, can recover.[7] Moreover, research strongly suggests that some degree of stress is actually healthy.[6] In fact, short-term events that are buffered by supportive adults enable children to develop the ability to self-regulate, learn from mistakes, and recover from disappointment.

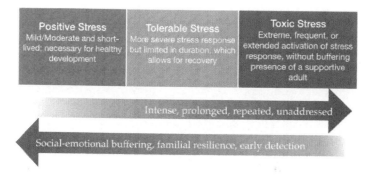

Based on work by the Center for the Developing Child,
Harvard University[4]

With their emphasis on movement, purposeful exploration, self-correction, and mindfulness, Montessori environments turn out to be ideal settings for developing long-term capacities for resilience and self-reliance.[3,8]

Mindfulness practice is increasingly recognized as a path toward adult wellbeing.[9] And as developmental psychologist Angeline Stoll Lillard explains, several elements of Montessori education exemplify mindfulness practices and produce positive cognitive as well as social outcomes.

Deep Concentration

Deep concentration is core to both Montessori pedagogy and mindfulness practice. Just as consistent practice of meditation enables a person to become more calm, aware, and generally self-regulated when not meditating,[10] Dr. Montessori discovered that children who engage in deep concentration on purposeful work emerge from that state more calm, self-regulated, and with higher social competencies. She referred to this process as *normalization*.[11]

Normalization is also, as psychologist Mihaly Csikszentmihalyi notes, a "flow" experience in which the child's sense of time – along with all its problems – falls away as she becomes one with her work.[8]

Sensorimotor Experiences

A more sensitive awareness of the connection between body and mind enables children, especially those exposed to trauma, to develop regulatory skills necessary for coping with stress. Both Montessori and mindfulness training deepen mind/body awareness through a focus on sensorimotor experiences. In mindfulness, such experiences may involve paying careful attention to how your hands feel when you wash dishes or how your mouth feels when you eat a strawberry. Similarly, when Practical Life activities like Handwashing is presented, the child is encouraged to take one's time and to attend to how the water and soap feels in the hands. Likewise, Sensorial work such as the Tasting Bottles provides opportunities for children to focus on the different flavors of sweet, sour, and bitter. Even Walking On The Line allows the child to feel his body and control his movement as he carefully walks with a small beanbag balanced on his head.

Nonjudgmental Environments

Montessori teachers are also taught to be non-judgmental so as to give the children the physical, psychological, and emotional space necessary to develop their sense of self. In mindfulness training, one is taught to not even judge one's own thoughts but, rather, to notice them.[12] Even the use of self-correcting materials in a classroom creates an environment where the children are free from constant judgment from authority.

In all, Montessori classrooms are places that, by design, help all children develop a mindfulness that allows them to effectively self-regulate and become resilient to the chronic adverse experiences that are beyond their control. And, as anyone who has ever spent time in a Montessori classroom knows, they are places where "very young children can and will focus attentively on meaningful work that incorporates body and mind. They also will be mindful of their actions when shown how to be so by attentive and loving adults" (p. 84).[2]

References

1. Chapman, D. P., Whitfield, C. L., Felitti, V. J., Dube, S. R., Edwards, V. J., & Anda, R. F. (2004). Adverse childhood experiences and the risk of depressive disorders in adulthood. *Journal of Affective Disorders, 82*(2), 217-225. ; Dube, S. R., Anda, R. F., Felitti, V. J., Chapman, D. P., Williamson, D. F., & Giles, W. H. (2001). Childhood abuse, household dysfunction, and the risk of attempted suicide throughout the life span: Findings from the adverse childhood experiences study. *JAMA, 286*(24), 3089-3096. doi: 10.1001/jama.286.24.3089; Felitti Md, F. V. J., Anda Md, M. S. R. F., Nordenberg Md, D., Williamson Ms, P. D. F., Spitz Ms, M. P. H. A. M., Edwards Ba, V., . . . Marks Md, M. P. H. J. S. (1998). Relationship of childhood abuse and household dysfunction to many of the leading causes of death in adults: The adverse childhood experiences (ACE) study. *American Journal of Preventive Medicine, 14*(4), 245-258. doi: http://dx.doi.org/10.1016/S0749-3797(98)00017-8

2. Lillard, A. S. (2011). Mindfulness practices in education: Montessori's approach. *Mindfulness, 2*(2), 78-85.

3. Sin, N. L., & Lyubomirsky, S. (2009). Enhancing well-being and alleviating depressive symptoms with positive psychology interventions: A practice-friendly meta-analysis. *Journal of clinical psychology, 65*(5), 467-487.

4. National Scientific Council on the Developing Child. (2005/2014). *Excessive Stress Disrupts the Architecture of the Developing Brain: Working Paper 3*. Updated Edition, Retrieved from www.developingchild.harvard.edu

5. Lupien, S. J., McEwen, B. S., Gunnar, M. R., & Heim, C. (2009). Effects of stress throughout the lifespan on the brain, behaviour and cognition. *Nature, 10*(6), 434-445. ; Shonkoff, J. P., Boyce, W., & McEwen, B. S. (2009). Neuroscience, molecular biology, and the childhood roots of health disparities: Building a new framework for health promotion and disease prevention. *JAMA, 301*(21), 2252-2259. doi: 10.1001/jama.2009.754; Osofsky, J. D. (1995). The effect of exposure to violence on young children. *American Psychologist, 50*(9), 782-788. doi: 10.1037/0003-066X.50.9.782

6. Shonkoff, J. P., Garner, A. S., Siegel, B. S., Dobbins, M. I., Earls, M. F., Garner, A. S., . . . Wood, D. L. (2012). The lifelong effects of early childhood adversity and toxic stress. *Pediatrics, 129*(1), e232-e246. doi: 10.1542/peds.2011-2663

7. Biglan, A., Flay, B. R., Embry, D. D., & Sandler, I. N. (2012). The critical role of nurturing environments for promoting human well-being. *American Psychologist, 67*(4), 257-271. doi: 10.1037/a0026796

8. Csikszentmihalyi, M. (2000). Positive psychology: The emerging paradigm. *NAMTA Journal, 25*(2), 5-25.

9. Brown, K. W., & Ryan, R. M. (2003). The benefits of being present: Mindfulness and its role in psychological well-being. *Journal of Personality and Social Psychology, 84*(4), 822-848. doi: 10.1037/0022-3514.84.4.822

10. Tang, Y. Y., Posner, M. I., & Rothbart, M. K. (2014). Meditation improves self-regulation over the life span. *Annals of the New York Academy of Sciences, 1307*(1), 104-11. doi: 10.1111/nyas.12227

11. Montessori, M. (1967). *The absorbent mind.* (1st ed.). New York, NY: Holt, Rinehart and Winston.

12. Kabat-Zinn, J. (2003). Mindfulness-based interventions in context: Past, present, and future. *Clinical Psychology: Science and Practice, 10*(2), 144-156.

BORN TO MOVE, PART 1: MOVEMENT AND COGNITION

Deborah Ely Budding, PhD
Laura Flores Shaw, MS

KEY POINTS

- According to neuroscientist Daniel Wolpert, "We have a brain for one reason, and one reason only: to produce adaptable and complex movements."

- In addition to the frontal cortex, more primitive brain regions – the basal ganglia and the cerebellum – are also involved in the circuitry for executive function (higher-level cognition).[8,9,10]

- Movement is linked to thought, and executive function is an extension of the motor control system.[3,12]

- It's important for educators to understand that because our brains were born to move, motor skill development precedes cognition. However, children are not born with well-developed motor and sensory systems, thus, those systems need to be trained.[12]

BORN TO MOVE, PART 1: MOVEMENT AND COGNITION

Deborah Ely Budding, PhD
Laura Flores Shaw, MS

It is high time that movement came to be regarded from a new point of view in educational theory. Especially in childhood we misunderstand its nature, and a number of mistaken ideas make us think of it as something less noble than it actually is. As a part of school life, which gives priority to the intellect, the role of movement has always been sadly neglected. When accepted there at all, it has only been under the heading of 'exercise,' 'physical education' or 'games.' But this is to overlook its close connection with the developing mind.

Maria Montessori
The Absorbent Mind (p. 136)

The Pink Tower is an iconic Montessori Sensorial material that helps children to (among other things) discern the differences in weights and sizes as each cube is carried to a working mat to be rebuilt. Even the process of weaving one's way through the busy classroom, cube in hand, while avoiding chairs, tables, toes of other children, and others' work mats is an important part of this material because it trains the child to move carefully and with purpose.

But all of this movement, from carrying the cubes to navigating one's way around the classroom, is not just essential to developing good coordination – it's essential to developing higher-level thinking.

BORN TO MOVE

In July 2011, neuroscientist Daniel Wolpert asked an audience of TEDGlobal participants this fundamental question: "Why do we and other animals have brains?"

As Wolpert suggests in his talk, most people may assume that we have brains in order to "perceive the world and think." But, he says, "That is completely wrong. We have a brain for one reason, and one reason only: to produce adaptable and complex movements."

This may not be immediately obvious. But if you really think about it, you may come to realize, as Wolpert states, that "movement is the only way you have of affecting the world around you." Everything we do to affect the world – speaking, writing, gesturing, etc. – requires contractions of muscles.

To illustrate his point, Wolpert talks about the life of the sea squirt, which philosopher Daniel Dennett describes in his book *Consciousness Explained*:

> The juvenile sea squirt wanders through the sea searching for a suitable rock or hunk of coral to cling to and make its home for life. For this task, it has a rudimentary nervous system. When it finds its spot and takes root, it doesn't need its brain anymore so it eats it! (It's rather like getting tenure.) (p. 177).[1]

Aside from the need to reevaluate tenure, what does it mean for education if the only reason we have brains is to "produce adaptable and complex movements?"

This article will be the first in a series to answer that question. But before we look at the answer, we need to look at how being born to move requires a new model of the brain.

THE VERTICAL MODEL OF THE BRAIN

Cognitive neuroscience has tended to focus on the cortex as the source of all cognitive activity and higher-order control over behavior. Neuroscience has also compartmentalized brain function into distinct domains: cognitive, attention/executive function, learning and memory, and sensory and motor.[2] However, this myopic and modular approach overlooks the interconnectedness of the brain and body, giving educators and clinicians limited understanding of the more complex relationships between the brain and behavior.[3]

What we know now through extensive fMRI research[4] is that more primitive brain regions – the basal ganglia and the cerebellum – which were once thought to only coordinate movement – are also involved in higher-level thinking and processes, typically referred to as executive function.[5] Here, we define executive function as "those functions [a person] employs to act independently [in her] own best interest as a whole, at any point in time, for the purpose of survival" (p. 506).[6,7]

Without the basal ganglia, the prefrontal cortex would not be able to select actions[8] or select what to attend to and maintain that attention.[9] And the cerebellum is the very foundation of executive function because it's the cerebellum that trains the highly regarded frontal lobes to predict by "thinking" about the potential outcomes of movement.[10]

What this means is that in order to better understand brain and behavior, it's not all about the frontal cortex. Instead, we need to view the brain vertically – from top to bottom – so that we can see all of the regions involved in the circuitry for executive function. For instance, the cerebro-cerebellar circuit involving word association is depicted (though very simply) in Figure 1.

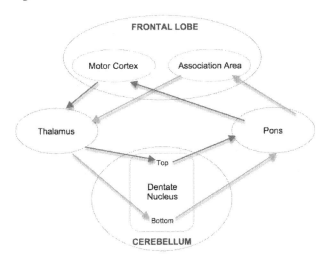

Figure One

Simplified cerebro-cerebellar circuit adapted from
Highnam, C. L., & Bleile, K. M. (2011)[11]

THE LINK BETWEEN MOVEMENT AND COGNITION

To effectively adapt to the environment, you have to learn how to manage both its predictable and unpredictable aspects. Predictable aspects require automatic, fixed, and routine responses. Unpredictable aspects require higher-order controlled responses, such as problem-solving and cognitive flexibility.[3]

Automatic behaviors used in predictable situations, however, aren't just relegated to motor movements like driving a car or brushing our teeth. They also involve:

- *cognitive behaviors* – reciting our multiplication tables or spelling our names;
- *social behaviors* – making eye contact or giving another person a turn to talk; and
- *emotional behaviors* – feeling good when we smell cookies or feeling attracted – or not – to someone.

The *higher-order control responses* also involve the same types of behaviors, but in a more complex way:

- *motor* – walking on uneven ground or driving in a foreign country;
- *cognitive* – planning and learning new skills or information;
- *social* – adapting to a new culture or learning someone's name; and
- *emotional* – holding back tears or resisting hitting a classmate.

Given the complexity of the world, to effectively function – or to have effective executive function – these two systems of automatic and higher-order responses must maintain a dynamic relationship so they can appropriately respond to a constantly changing environment. If you use the wrong system in a situation, like when you automatically speed through a page of equations without realizing that the signs of the operations are different, you're more vulnerable to mistakes, and you may not learn from those mistakes, leaving you disabled in that context.

Development of the automatic and higher-order response systems unfolds in a predictable way. First, the child senses and moves (i.e., the suck reflex). And, through moving she discovers objects (like a mother's breast) and learns about their properties (that a breast gives milk); thus, sensing, movement, and cognition coexist. Finally, her newly learned behavior becomes automatic, making cognition subordinate to movement because she no longer needs to consciously think about that movement to achieve her objective.[6]

Essentially, movement is linked to thought, and executive function is an extension of the motor control system.[3,12]

So what does this mean for educators?

IMPLICATIONS FOR EDUCATION
Sensorimotor Training

It's important for educators to understand that because our brains were born to move, motor skill development precedes cognition. However, children are not born with well-developed motor and sensory systems.[12] And the research shows that when children have unusual difficulty performing motor skills early in their development, they frequently have later problems with working memory and academic learning. In fact, children with learning disabilities generally have poor motor skills.[13] All of this means that educators must provide environments rich in sensorimotor materials – materials that train the senses and motor abilities.

Maria Montessori, of course, understood this. Remember when we said earlier that sensing, movement, and cognition coexist? Dr. Montessori said the same thing over 100 years ago:

> If we have a brain, sense organs and muscles, all these must co-operate. The system must exert itself in all its parts, none of them being neglected. We want, let us say, to excel in brain-power, but to succeed in this we must include the other sides also (p. 140).[14]

So she designed her curriculum knowing that the senses and movement had to be trained (sadly, this is not understood in conventional education[15]). One of the purposes of the Practical Life activities in a primary (ages 3-6) classroom is to refine movement. And the Sensorial materials are specifically designed to both train the senses and develop motor control (among other things, like develop the mathematical mind – but that's another white paper).

For example, the white paper *Reading and the Brain: Developing the Reading Circuit* (this volume), describes how the Sensorial materials are used to promote audio and visual acuity to prepare children for reading (among other things). Additionally, movement of the fingers to trace the cursive Sandpaper Letters facilitates better learning of letter sounds, which is necessary for decoding and later reading skills.[16]

Movement, however, doesn't stop at preschool in Montessori. You'll often find elementary children engaging in behaviors usually frowned upon in conventional classrooms, like running down the halls or jumping around the classroom. These children aren't being rowdy and disobedient. Instead, they're learning about verbs by acting out their actions as noted on the Verb Command Cards. Even adolescents spend a lot of time away from desks, using their knowledge of math and engineering to build elaborate watering structures for their chickens or other farm animals. In Montessori education, movement is important at all levels.

Developing Cognitive Flexibility

Another educational implication for movement's link to cognition is development of *cognitive flexibility* – the ability to generalize across circumstances and to extrapolate information outside of the current context. Cognitive flexibility is an important component of executive function,[17] and Montessori provides scaffolding for its unfolding in a natural manner.

For instance, when a child is presented with the Table Washing activity at approximately age three, he is shown how to make medium circular movements with his arm to sponge down the tabletop. This circular motion is indirect preparation for cursive writing. He is also shown to start sponging from left to right, which is more indirect preparation for writing and reading. So when it comes time for children to start reading and writing they already have embodied within them the knowledge of left to right sequencing and how it feels to write in circular motions. In fact, all of the Practical Life materials train the children to do things in a left to right sequence. They also help the children to sequence behaviors and thoughts as children learn the many steps involved in each exercise.

Some students who are not neurotypical, however, may have difficulty independently and intuitively applying this embodied knowledge. For those students, simply pointing out that writing feels similar to washing a tabletop or that reading and writing involves always starting from left to write, just like Table Washing and other activities, can be enough to help these students recognize and apply that embodied knowledge in their current context of learning.

THE FINAL MESSAGE

Dr. Montessori best expressed what educators need to know about the link between movement and cognition:

> When mental development is under discussion, there are many who say, "How does movement come into it? We are talking about the mind." And when we think of intellectual activity, we always imagine people sitting still, motionless. But mental development *must* be connected with movement and be dependent on it. It is vital that educational theory and practice should become informed by this idea (pgs. 141-142; emphasis in original).[14]

References

1. Dennett, D. C. (1991). Consciousness explained (1st ed.). Boston, MA: Little, Brown and Co.

2. Toates, F. (2004). Cognition, motivation, emotion and action: A dynamic and vulnerable interdependence. *Applied Animal Behaviour Science, 86*(3–4), 173-204. doi: http://dx.doi.org/10.1016/j.applanim.2004.02.010

3. Koziol, L. F., & Budding, D. E. (2009). *Subcortical structures and cognition: Implications for neuropsychological assessment.* New York, NY: Springer.

4. Küper, M., Dimitrova, A., Thürling, M., Maderwald, S., Roths, J., Elles, H. G., . . . Timmann, D. (2011). Evidence for a motor and a non-motor domain in the human dentate nucleus — An fMRI study. *NeuroImage, 54*(4), 2612-2622. doi: http://dx.doi.org/10.1016/j.neuroimage.2010.11.028; Habas, C. (2010). Functional imaging of the deep cerebellar nuclei: A review. *The Cerebellum, 9*(1), 22-28. doi: http://dx.doi.org/10.1007/s12311-009-0119-3

5. Schmahmann, J. D., & Caplan, D. (2006). Cognition, emotion and the cerebellum. *Brain, 129,* 290-292. doi: 10.1093/brain/awh729; Diamond, A. (2000). Close interrelation of motor development and cognitive development and of the cerebellum and prefrontal cortex. *Child Development, 71,* 44-56.

6. Koziol, L. F., Budding, D. E., & Chidekel, D. (2012). From movement to thought: executive function, embodied cognition, and the cerebellum. *The Cerebellum, 11*(2), 505-525.

7. Miller, R. (2007). *A theory of the basal ganglia and their disorders.* Boca Raton, FL: CRC Press.

8. Seger, C. A. (2008). How do the basal ganglia contribute to categorization? Their roles in generalization, response selection, and learning via feedback. *Neuroscience & Biobehavioral Reviews, 32*(2), 265-278. doi: http://dx.doi.org/10.1016/j.neubiorev.2007.07.010

9. Frank, M. J., Santamaria, A., O'Reilly, R. C., & Willcutt, E. (2007). Testing computational models of dopamine and noradrenaline dysfunction in attention deficit//hyperactivity disorder. *Neuropsychopharmacology, 32*(7), 1583-1599.

10. Ito, M. (2008). Control of mental activities by internal models in the cerebellum. *Nature Reviews Neuroscience, 9*(4), 304-313. doi: 10.1038/nrn2332

11. Highnam, C. L., & Bleile, K. M. (2011). Language in the cerebellum. *American Journal of Speech-Language Pathology, 20*(4), 337-347. doi: 10.1044/1058-0360(2011/10-0096)

12. Koziol, L. F., Budding, D. E., & Chidekel, D. (2010). Adaptation, expertise, and giftedness: Towards an understanding of cortical, subcortical, and cerebellar network contributions. *The Cerebellum, 9*(4), 499-529. doi: http://dx.doi.org/10.1007/s12311-010-0192-7; Cotterill, R. M. J. (2001). Cooperation of the basal ganglia, cerebellum, sensory cerebrum and hippocampus: possible implications for cognition,

consciousness, intelligence and creativity. *Progress in Neurobiology, 64*(1), 1-33. doi: http://dx.doi.org/10.1016/S0301-0082(00)00058-7

13. Westendorp, M., Hartman, E., Houwen, S., Smith, J., & Visscher, C. (2011). The relationship between gross motor skills and academic achievement in children with learning disabilities. *Research in Developmental Disabilities, 32*(6), 2773-2779. doi: http://dx.doi.org/10.1016/j.ridd.2011.05.032

14. Montessori, M. (1967). *The absorbent mind* (1st ed.). New York: Holt, Rinehart and Winston.

15. Lillard, A. S. (2007). *Montessori: The science behind the genius.* New York, NY: Oxford University Press.

16. Bara, F., Gentaz, E., Colé, P., & Sprenger-Charolles, L. (2004). The visuo-haptic and haptic exploration of letters increases the kindergarten-children's understanding of the alphabetic principle. *Cognitive Development, 19*(3), 433-449. doi: http://dx.doi.org/10.1016/j.cogdev.2004.05.003

17. Anderson, P. (2002). Assessment and development of executive function (EF) during childhood. *Child Neuropsychology, 8*(2), 71.

MONTESSORI AND PLAY

Laura Flores Shaw, MS

KEY POINTS

- Though articles abound in the media extolling the virtues of play on children's cognitive development while demonizing work,[1] these articles rarely define play, and they only seem to define work as the didactic instruction found in conventional schools.

- Within the research literature, there is the overall construct of *playful learning*, which is broken down into *free play* and *guided play*.[2] The latter benefits children's learning while the former does not.[6]

- *Pretend play* does not foster creativity, better problem solving, and higher intelligence; nor does it foster better social and emotional competencies.[6]

- Dr. Maria Montessori initially thought children needed toys, but the children showed her otherwise, so she removed them from the environment.[11]

- An examination of the broad *playful learning* construct and Montessori education found that the two have much in common: both have an overarching structure, free choice, peer interaction, materials specific to the developmental stage, a lack of extrinsic rewards, and just plain fun.[14] These elements are also present during pretend play.[6]

- The dichotomy of play versus work is false, as it fails to consider how the two actually overlap.[16]

MONTESSORI AND PLAY

Laura Flores Shaw, MS

Had…children chosen instead to play with toys, a very different educational system would have been developed.

Angeline Lillard, PhD
Montessori: The Science Behind the Genius

When I was the head of a Montessori school many years ago, a prospective parent who came to tour the school greeted me by saying, "I'm only here because my husband went to a Montessori school as a child, and he insisted I visit. But I don't believe in 'work' for children. I believe in 'play.'"

Needless to say the meeting did not go well.

Her assumption that work is bad while play is good for children kept her from seeing what was really happening in the classroom. But who can blame her? Articles abound in the media extolling the virtues of play on children's cognitive development while demonizing work.[1] What no one seems to notice, however, is that these articles rarely define play, and they only seem to define work as the didactic instruction found in conventional schools. But when we really examine the constructs of play and work, we see that there is far more to this picture than "play is good" and "work is bad" for young children – especially within a Montessori context. In fact, we find that the dichotomy of work and play as usually presented in the mainstream media by well-meaning child advocates is actually a false one.

WHAT IS PLAY?

Play is a construct that is likely to mean different things to different people. For parents, play may bring to mind children frolicking through fields, hanging from trees, playing in mud, and generally just doing whatever one wants. But for researchers who must actually define their constructs to clarify what they're studying, play is more complex than that.

Within the research literature, there is the overall construct of *playful learning*, which is broken down into *free play* and *guided play*.[2] Free play involves pretending (which is discussed in detail later), playing with objects and/or peers, rough-and-tumble play with very little adult control, and no extrinsic rewards. Guided play, on the other hand, falls on a continuum and involves adult guidance that promotes academic knowledge through activities that feel like play rather than the I-want-to-poke-my-own-eyes-out-because-I-have-to-sit-still-and-listen-to-the-adult form of didactic instruction. This continuum is also based on the amount of guidance a teacher provides. For instance, some teachers may only provide guidance via specific materials in the environment, while other teachers may provide materials and still lead all playful activities. But there is that wonderful middle ground, as Fisher, et al. (2011)[2] state:

> Teachers play a unique role in guided play experiences. They can sensitively guide learning, creating flexible, interest-driven experiences that encourage children's autonomy/control over the process (p. 343).

Further support for this wonderful middle ground on the guided play continuum comes from two meta-analyses conducted in 2011 examining 164 studies of *discovery learning*. These analyses showed that *unassisted discovery*, as it occurs in free play (wherein the teacher provides no actual guidance in the learning process), doesn't benefit students. However, *guided discovery* involving more teacher scaffolding and feedback (which can come directly from the materials or other students and not the teacher) does benefit students.[3]

Overall, play is a broad construct, and what the research shows is that free play doesn't benefit children's learning. Does that mean children should not be allowed time for free play? No. But it does mean that developing a "curriculum" around free play won't provide children with opportunities to practice purposeful sensorimotor skills that need to become automatic so that later deeper learning can occur.[4] We can't just tell children, "Play until you're six, but then you need to get down to business" when we haven't provided opportunities for them to gain the sensorimotor skills necessary for literacy and numeracy. Instead, we need to provide those opportunities for learning in a way that feels playful.

Pretend Play

A common concern parents have with respect to Montessori is that the classrooms lack a dress-up corner where the children can engage in pretend play. Montessori children are also encouraged to use the materials as presented rather than pretending, for instance, that the Red Rods (which provide indirect preparation for mathematics and directly train visual discrimination of differences in length) are ski poles. Again, this concern is understandable due to the plethora of articles claiming that pretend play fosters creativity, better problem solving, and higher intelligence.[5]

However, careful analyses of 40 years worth of research on pretend play and its purported benefits shows that "the evidence that pretend play enhances creativity is not convincing" (p. 8).[6] These analyses also showed that construction play (such as block building) correlated with better problem-solving while pretend play did not (score one for the Pink Tower!). In fact, when children assign meaning to an object through pretend play, that meaning can interfere with understanding the object's true meaning and use, suggesting that pretend play doesn't improve problem-solving skills.[7] Meaning interference is also why we don't want the children pretending the Red Rods are ski poles as this can interfere with their ability to embody the concept of length.

Finally, while there is a relationship between pretend play and intelligence, the direction of that relationship is unclear, so the claim that pretend play raises intelligence is unsubstantiated at this point.[6]

But what about pretend play's effect on social and emotional skills? Surely pretending increases these competencies as children engage in role-playing games.

It is true that researchers have claimed that both pretending alone and in a group contribute to social and emotional competencies because they allow children to play out their own social and emotional issues, and they can practice their negotiation skills.[8] But as developmental psychologist Jerome Kagan points out, "scientists who study human nature...usually have a favored purpose in mind before they begin their work" (p. 4),[9] and for many, play may be a good and necessary purpose for children. When analyzing the actual studies, however, they don't confirm the claims that pretending contributes to social and emotional competencies. Overall, the studies show inconsistent correlations, which shows that a causal link between pretend play and social and emotional competencies doesn't exist.[6]

(Of course, correlation is not causation; however, if a number of studies consistently show correlational relationships between two variables in the same direction, then one can begin to make a case for causation – though very, very cautiously.)

MONTESSORI AND WORK

Dr. Montessori was fully aware that psychologists assumed that play was vital to young children's development. In a lecture presented in London in 1946, she stated:

> Psychologists have attached great importance to [play] and make vague statements – that children play at this age – that they develop their character through play. They also say that the individuality of the children is revealed in their play (p.151).[10]

In fact, as Dr. Montessori explains in *The Secret of Childhood*, toys were available to the children in the first Montessori school, but the children rarely chose to play with them:

> Since they never freely chose these toys, I realized that in the life of a child play is perhaps something of little importance which he undertakes for lack of something better to do. A child feels that he has something of greater moment to do than to be engaged in such trivial occupations. He regards play as we would regard a game of chess or bridge. These are pleasant occupations for hours of leisure, but they would become painful if we were obliged to pursue them at great length. When we have some important business to do, bridge is forgotten. And since a child always has some important thing at hand, he is not particularly interested in playing (p. 122).[11]

Unlike other educational reformers who sought to impose their views and ideologies upon children, Dr. Montessori developed her method through systematic observation of children. And so while she initially thought that children needed toys just as the psychologists did, the children showed her otherwise, so she removed them from the environment.

In fact, there were two other significant incidents wherein students showed their preference for Montessori's purposeful materials over toys or free play. In both situations, the children had been locked out of their classrooms without a teacher. The first incident occurred at the first

Montessori school in Rome, while the second occurred at the Panama-Pacific International Exposition in San Francisco in 1915 where a glass classroom was set up so people could watch the children work. During both of these lockout incidents, the children could have easily chosen to stay outside and play. Instead, they chose to find a way into their classrooms so they could work. And the teachers weren't even present.[12]

I have witnessed firsthand children's preference for working in their classroom over free play. At the Montessori school I once administered, we decided one year to try running a summer camp for the primary (ages 3-6) students instead of summer school so we could give the teachers a long break. To maintain a Montessori atmosphere during camp, the children could choose what they wanted to do, and the activities included crafts, toys, and free play. A couple of weeks into the summer, we started hearing from the children and their parents that the children were bored, and they wanted to go back to working with the materials in their classrooms. We never ran another camp.

Ultimately, frolicking in mud and hanging from trees may seem like the idyllic early childhood experience, but that's only because we adults tend to perceive "work" as a pejorative term as we spend our work days counting down to the weekend. Montessori children, however, don't because their work brings them higher affect, energy, and intrinsic motivation.[13] Work feels good.

In fact, an examination of the broad *playful learning* construct and Montessori education found that the two have much in common: both have an overarching structure, free choice, peer interaction, materials specific to the developmental stage, a lack of extrinsic rewards, and just plain fun.[14] These elements are also present during pretend play.[6] This means that "work" in Montessori classrooms feels like play to children. In fact, it might even feel better than pretend play because the children actually get to use real tools and materials!

A FALSE DICHOTOMY

When educators advocate for play in early childhood education, they are fighting against the adult-centered, didactic instruction found in conventional schools – and with good reason. Forcing children to sit and listen to adults for long periods is not developmentally appropriate. I'm not even sure it's appropriate for adults.[15]

But this dichotomy of play and work fails to consider how the two actually overlap. As education professor Joan Goodman states:

> Absent clear criteria, play comes to be defined by its opposite – work – and the large overlap is lost" (p. 185).[16]

In her article *"Work" Versus "Play" and Early Childhood Care*, Goodman articulates how the research literature generally distinguishes work from play, but she also shows their great overlap. First, play is considered to be fun, easy, and pleasurable, while work is unpleasant and effortful. However, play can also require tremendous effort (as when one plays hard) and work can feel quite pleasurable – especially when in a state of flow, wherein you're fully immersed in what you're doing and time just seems to fly by.[17]

Second, play is about freedom while work is about constraint, obliging "us to discipline our behavior, follow rules, do what the conventional standard demands" (p. 185).[16] But Goodman reminds us that children often create rules for their own play activities, as they prefer a sense of order.

Third, play is about process while work is focused on outcome. But this distinction is also erroneous. Play, like work, has an endpoint, and children often evaluate their own products of play.

Finally, play is considered to be intrinsically motivated and self-chosen, whereas work is extrinsically motivated and imposed upon us by some outside authority. This means "the very same activity . . . can be play or work," depending upon whether or not the person is obliged to do it (p. 186). In a Montessori context, this means that all of the classroom activities can be considered play since it is the children who choose what to do!

Because work feels like play within a Montessori context, those students learn that "work" means something one wants do. And as Goodman states:

> What seems to be the case, then, is that the criteria of play that most distinguishes it from work – its self-chosen intrinsically motivated quality – is also the quality that should imbue work; work in school and work in the work place for that matter (p. 188).[16]

Hopefully, Montessori students' experience of work as self-chosen and intrinsically motivated will lead them to spend their adult years doing work that is meaningful to them rather than spending those years counting the days down to the weekend.

References

1. Kohn, D. (2015). Let the kids learn through play. *The New York Times.* http://www.nytimes.com/2015/05/17/opinion/sunday/let-the-kids-learn-through-play.html?_r=0; Hamilton, J. (2014). Scientists say child's play helps build a better brain. *NPR.* http://www.npr.org/sections/ed/2014/08/06/336361277/scientists-say-childs-play-helps-build-a-better-brain

2. Fisher, K., Hirsh-Pasek, K., Golinkoff, R. M., Singer, D. G., & Berk, L. (2011). Playing around in school: Implications for learning and educational policy. *The Oxford handbook of the development of play*, 341-362.

3. Alfieri, L., Brooks, P. J., Aldrich, N. J., & Tenenbaum, H. R. (2011). Does discovery-based instruction enhance learning? *Journal of Educational Psychology, 103*(1), 1-18. doi: 10.1037/a0021017

4. Dehaene, S. (2009). *Reading in the brain: The new science of how we read.* New York, NY: Viking; Jordan, N. C., Kaplan, D., Locuniak, M. N., & Ramineni, C. (2007). Predicting first-grade math achievement from developmental number sense trajectories. *Learning Disabilities Research & Practice, 22*(1), 36-46. ; Jordan, N. C., Kaplan, D., Ramineni, C., & Locuniak, M. N. (2009). Early math matters: Kindergarten number competence and later mathematics outcomes. *Developmental Psychology, 45*(3), 850-867. doi: 10.1037/a0014939; Seung-Hee, S., & Meisels, S. J. (2006). The relationship of young children's motor skills to later reading and math achievement. *Merrill-Palmer Quarterly, 52*(4), 755-778.

5. Copple, C., & Bredekamp, S. (2009). *Developmentally appropriate practice in early childhood programs serving children from birth through age 8.* Washington, DC: National Association for the Education of Young Children; Hurwitz, S. C. (2002). To be successful--Let them play! *Childhood Education, 79*(2), 101-102. ; Kaufman, B. K. (2012). The need for pretend play in child development. *Psychology Today.* https://www.psychologytoday.com/blog/beautiful-minds/201203/the-need-pretend-play-in-child-development

6. Lillard, A. S., Lerner, M. D., Hopkins, E. J., Dore, R. A., Smith, E. D., & Palmquist, C. M. (2013). The impact of pretend play on children's development: A review of the evidence. *Psychological Bulletin, 139*(1), 1-34. doi: 10.1037/a0029321

7. DeLoache, J. S. (2000). Dual representation and young children's use of scale models. *Child Development, 71*(2), 329-338.

8. Stagnitti, K., & Unsworth, C. (2000). The importance of pretend play in child development: An occupational therapy perspective. *The British Journal of Occupational Therapy, 63*(3), 121-127.; Harris, P. L. (2000). *The work of the imagination.* Oxford, England: Blackwell Publishing.

9. Kagan, J. (1984). The nature of the child. New York, NY: Basic Books.

10. Montessori, M. (1946/2012). Lecture 21: Work and play. In A. Haines (Ed.), *The 1946 London lectures.* Amsterdam, The Netherlands: Montessori-Pierson Publishing Company.

11. Montessori, M. (1966). *The secret of childhood* (S. J. M. Joseph Costelloe, Trans.). New York, NY: Ballantine Books.

12. Lillard, A. S. (2005). *Montessori: The science behind the genius.* New York, NY: Oxford University Press.

13. Csikszentmihalyi, M., & LeFevre, J. (1989). Optimal experience in work and leisure. *Journal of Personality and Social Psychology, 56*(5), 815.

14. Lillard, A. S. (2013). Playful learning and Montessori education. *American Journal of Play, 5*(2), 157-186.

15. Prince, M. (2004). Does active learning work? A review of the research. *Journal of Engineering Education, 93*, 223-232.

16. Goodman, J. (1994). "Work" versus "play" and early childhood care. *Child and Youth Care Forum, 23*(3), 177-196. doi: 10.1007/BF02209227

17. Csikszentmihalyi, M. (1991). *Flow: The psychology of optimal experience* (1st ed.). New York, NY: HarperPerennial.

MONTESSORI AND THE SYSTEMS WORLDVIEW

Laura Flores Shaw, MS

KEY POINTS

- Montessori education fosters a systems view of the world, which is necessary for the sustainability of our planet and, hence, our species.

- Recognizing the need to educate children about the "complex interdependence between human needs and the natural environment, between socio-economic development and culture, and between the local and the global," the UN declared the 2005-2014 decade as the Decade of Education for Sustainable Development (p. 12).[7] But education for sustainability is less of a curriculum and more of a mindset – a mindset that thinks in terms of systems rather than mechanisms.[8]

- Current researchers of education for sustainability are proposing educational paradigms that strongly resemble Montessori education.[8]

MONTESSORI AND THE SYSTEMS WORLDVIEW

Laura Flores Shaw, MS

Here is an essential principle of education: to teach details is to bring confusion;
to establish the relationship between things is to bring knowledge.

Maria Montessori
The Absorbent Mind

A previously published white paper proposed that Montessori is *the* educational method for developing the skills necessary to be successful in the 21st century knowledge economy.[1] Specifically, it argued that the accelerating rate of both technological and social innovation will require our children to "reinvent" themselves more than once during their lifetimes; thus children need more than anything to be able to think creatively, which Montessori fosters more so than other educational methods.[2] This means that choosing a Montessori education for your children sets them up for greater potential of economic success as adults, more so than conventional education, which is still situated within the factory model framework generated by the now defunct industrial economy.[3]

But there is another and, arguably, even more important reason why Montessori is *the* educational method for the 21st century: Montessori education fosters a systems view of the world, which is necessary for the sustainability of our planet and, hence, our species.

The Systems Worldview and Education

The problems that plague our planet and our global society[4] cannot be solved with a reductionistic worldview that fails to see the large and

36

complex systems in which those problems are situated. As John Sterman, director of the MIT System Dynamics Group states:

> ...the unsustainability of our society arises because we treat the world as unlimited and problems unconnected when we live on a finite "spaceship Earth" in which "there is no away" and "everything is connected to everything else" (p. 23).[5]

Thus, what is needed is a systems worldview that allows one to perceive the world "in terms of connectedness, relationships, and context" (p. 10).[6] This is different from the mechanistic perspective, which views the world and its inhabitants as machines that can be understood by the arrangement and movement of their individual parts. This view dominated scientific thinking for 300 years until advances in organismic biology in the early 20th century showed that reducing complex structures to their smallest parts couldn't account for properties that emerge from the interactions of those parts.

Yet the mechanistic view still permeates our thinking as its 300-year dominance led us to organizing our institutions into silos. Governments, companies, and universities are organized by departments, and schools break down their curricula into single subjects.[5] This siloing then leads to viewing problems of economy, society, and environment as separate when, in fact, they "are not separate domains to be traded off against one another" (p. 26).[5] Rather, they are all interrelated.

Recognizing the need to educate children about the "complex interdependence between human needs and the natural environment, between socio-economic development and culture, and between the local and the global," the UN declared the 2005-2014 decade as the Decade of Education for Sustainable Development (p. 12).[7] But education for sustainability is less of a curriculum and more of a mindset – a mindset that thinks in terms of systems rather than mechanisms.[8] And for this mindset to occur within conventional education, the current mindset underlying that system needs to radically change.

In her paper, *What is an Education for Sustainable Development Supposed to Achieve—A Question of What, How and Why*, education researcher Maria Hofman beautifully summarizes a new educational paradigm proposed by professor of sustainability education, Stephen Sterling:

> A policy change should develop education from being seen as a product to being described as an ongoing developmental process that develops potential and capacity throughout life at both the individual level and

societal level through lifelong learning. Such learning requires a change in the methodology and practice within education. Instead of education limited to instruction and knowledge transfer, the change should result in education being developed into a dynamic, activity-based and participatory training based on generating knowledge and meaning in relation to the circumstances in local society and the world. Problem solution in such education is thus based on real events (p. 224).[8]

That paradigm sounds like Montessori.

Montessori: Designed With A Systems Worldview

For over 100 years, Montessori has been fostering a systems worldview for children through both its structure and curriculum.

In terms of structure, the environments are designed such that the children experience both individualism and interrelatedness. There is (generally) only one of every material in the environment, so should a child break a material, she learns that this affects the other children as well since they, too, will not be able to use it until it is replaced. The classrooms also have processes in place – processes determined by the children (depending upon their age). These processes help a classroom full of mixed-aged children simultaneously engaged in different activities to function smoothly. Not adhering to these processes adversely affects the classroom's functioning, and the other children will be sure to notice it. In both incidences, the child is never shamed. Instead, discussions occur amongst the children through class meetings where they learn to support one another and democratically decide any necessary change. Overall, this structure allows the children to actively experience how their actions and choices affect the larger system that is their classroom community.

The curriculum also fosters a systems worldview, particularly the Cosmic Education curriculum, which begins in elementary. Dr. Montessori believed that every living creature has a cosmic task that contributes to "the upkeep of the earth and of maintaining harmony on it" (p. 129).[9] But the cosmic task of humans, due to their intelligence and ability to modify nature, goes beyond mere upkeep and maintenance of nature. Instead, their task is to use their abilities to contribute to the formation of a harmonious society. Thus, Cosmic Education is the "universal syllabus" designed to foster that task. Dr. Montessori describes the syllabus as follows:

In the universal syllabus of studies to which the new generations must apply themselves, all the items of culture must be connected as different aspects of the knowledge of the world and the cosmos. Astronomy, geography, geology, biology, physics, chemistry are but details of one whole. It is their relation to one another that urges interest from a centre towards its ramifications (p. 131).[9]

Specifically, the syllabus includes five *great lessons*, each of which gives an overview of an entire subject area, and *key lessons*, which are lessons involving a specific subject area or a particular skill or principle emerging from a great lesson.[10]

The first great lesson introduces the formation of the universe, the solar system, and earth. The second and third lessons introduce the evolution of life on earth and the essential characteristics of humans. The fourth and fifth great lessons focus on the invention of communication through alphabetic and numerical symbols.

The key lessons emerge from the great lessons and cover the discipline areas of language, mathematics (including geometry and measurement), history, geography, science (with biology as a distinct study area), creative arts, physical education, and non-native languages. These lessons are intentionally brief, providing just enough information so the children can independently explore a topic in greater depth.

When the key lessons are given, multiple subject areas may be discussed. For instance, when introducing geometry to the children, the teacher will first tell a story about how farmers who lived along the Nile in ancient Egypt used knotted ropes to reconfigure their property lines after the river's flooding washed away their property markers. Knowing the exact measurement of their land was necessary, as the famers were required to pay the Pharaoh taxes based on the amount of land they owned. At this point in the story, the teacher invites three children (there would likely be no more than 4 children attending the lesson) to hold a two-knotted rope – one child at each of the two knots while the third child holds the ends of the rope together, forming a right-angled scalene triangle.

Then, with great enthusiasm, the teacher briefly introduces Thales, Pythagoras, Plato, Euclid, and Archimedes. And the children are told how Abraham Lincoln mastered the first four books of Euclid's *The Elements* to train his mind to reason logically. This key lesson ties geometry to Egyptian, Greek, and American history, prompting the children to reflect upon geometry's historical development. It also encourages them to think about geometry's practical application across domains, which may further inspire them to study one aspect of the lesson in greater depth.

Clearly, Cosmic Education is not focused on knowledge transfer; rather, it is "dynamic, activity-based and participatory training based on generating knowledge and meaning in relation to the circumstances in local society and the world" (p. 131)[9] – exactly what professor of sustainability education, Stephen Sterling, thinks education should be.

So while it's important that we equip our children to be economically independent adults, we must think beyond that if we want our children's children and their children to live more harmonious lives – or even just live. And many researchers today think that education is the vehicle to developing a systems worldview so the problem solvers of future generations can behave in a way that sustains our planet and our species.

Maria Montessori thought this, too.

References

1. Flores, M. A. (2015). Education for the 21st century economy. *The Montessori White Papers, 1*, 1-6.

2. Shaw, L. F. (2015). Montessori and creativity. *The Montessori White Papers, 1*, 7-13. ; Besançon, M., & Lubart, T. (2008). Differences in the development of creative competencies in children schooled in diverse learning environments. *Learning and Individual Differences, 18*(4), 381-389. doi: http://dx.doi.org/10.1016/j.lindif.2007.11.009; Besançon, M., Lubart, T., & Barbot, B. (2013). Creative giftedness and educational opportunities. *Educational & Child Psychology, 30*(2), 79-88.

3. Shaw, L. F. (2015). Education doesn't need to reformd - It needs to be transformed. *Huffington Post*. http://www.huffingtonpost.com/laura-flores-shaw/education-doesnt-need-to-_b_7558044.html

4. McGrew, A. (1992). A global society? In S. Hall, D. Held & A. McGrew (Eds.), *Modernity and its futures: Understanding modern societies, Book IV* (pp. 466-503). UK: Polity Publisher.

5. Sterman, J. D. (2012). Sustaining sustainability: Creating a systems science in a fragmented academy and polarized world. In M. P. Weinstein & R. E. Turner (Eds.), *Sustainability science: The emerging paradigm and the urban environment* (pp. 21-58): Springer

6. Capra, F., & Luisi, P. L. (2014). *The systems view of life: A unifying vision*. India: Cambridge University Press.

7. UNESCO. (2005). Paper presented at the Globalization and education for sustainable development: Sustaining the future, Nagoya, Japan.

8. Hofman, M. (2015). What is an education for sustainable development supposed to achieve— A question of what, how and why. *Journal of Education for Sustainable Development, 9*(2), 213-228. doi: 10.1177/0973408215588255

9.   Montessori, M. (1946/1997). Keys to the world: Man and the world: "Cosmic education" *Basic ideas of Montessori's educational theory* (pp. 128-133). Oxford, England: Clio Press.

10.   Montessori National Curricululm. (2012). Montessori national curriculum for the second plane of development from six to twelve years. *NAMTA, 37*(1), 83-242.

ABOUT WHITE PAPER PRESS

White Paper Press is a think tank specializing in translating scientific research into terms that allow people to make informed decisions about their lives. We are committed to understanding what science knows now (knowing that knowledge may change tomorrow) and to fostering critical thought.

As a social venture, White Paper Press seeks to stimulate change to accepted schemas and frameworks that do not best serve our society or us as individual citizens. With our first publication, *The Montessori White Papers*, we challenge the traditional concept of school.

52190490R00033

Made in the USA
San Bernardino, CA
13 August 2017